MW01235550

Spiritual INSPIRATIONS

To. J. Anthony Brown

Carl B Pugh

9. 15-22

Charleston, SC
www.PalmettoPublishing.com

Spiritual Inspirations Volume 1
Copyright © 2022 by Carol B Pugh

First Edition

Hardcover ISBN: 979-8-8229-0216-9
Paperback ISBN: 979-8-8229-0217-6

Spiritual INSPIRATIONS
Volume 1

Carol B Pugh

THIS BOOK IS DEDICATED TO ALL
OF GOD'S PEOPLE WHO NEED A
HEALING.

May God be with you.

CONTENTS

. . . .

PART 5:
INSPIRING

PART 6:
LOVING

PART 7:
HEALINGS

PART 1:
Warnings

JEALOUSY

The things that people won't do.

Jealousy is something else.

Thinking the world revolves around you.

I'm jealous and selfish.

If Jesus showed his face,

I would turn my back on him.

I can't put anyone else first

because I'm number one.

I'm jealous and selfish.

I don't know how to care about anyone else.

I left Jesus a long time ago.

I'm jealous and selfish.

I am always looking for a way to get over.

So, you'd better watch out for me.

I'm jealous and selfish.

When you see me, you'd better step to the side.

Because I might just walk all over you.

I've got my blinders on.

I can't see anyone else but myself.

I'm jealous and selfish.

. . . .

I will pose for a picture.

I want you to capture all of me.

I've got to show off.

I'm jealous and selfish.

When you meet someone who cannot
appreciate you for you,

Taking your kindness for weakness, that
person is not for you.

Jealous and self-centered, that's who I am.

A GATHERING
OF A STORM

Since the beginning of time, the people
haven't been right.

Even the angels in heaven weren't right.

There is a storm rising; get right.

We are living in our last days.

The world doesn't even know what is right.

There is a storm rising; get right.

People are killing people for no reason.

Too much crime, too little time.

There is a storm rising; get right.

Kids are defying their parents.

. . . .

3

Not listening and doing whatever.

There is a storm rising; get right.

Even the weather doesn't even know it's season.

Winters are like summers. Springs like falls.

There is a storm rising; get right.

How much time do you think we have left?

Who knows the date of the return of the Messiah?

There is a storm rising; get right.

I don't know about you.

I am going to take this time to get right.

There is a storm rising; get right.

Question: Will you be right when the storm comes?

The return of Jesus Christ.

There is a storm rising; get right.

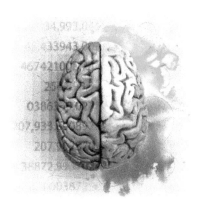

THINKING LIKE JESUS

I tried to think like Jesus. Isn't that something.

I had gotten beside myself.

Believing something that I should not believe.

Thinking like Jesus, but not.

I could think with both sides of my brain at the same time.

I was highly intelligent, but my mind couldn't think that high.

I was getting in my own way.

Jesus is at a different level.

Thinking like Jesus, but not.

. . . .

I was good at thinking outside the box.

I wanted to take my mind to a higher level.

I craved knowledge.

My mind didn't even know how to shut itself down.

My mind was always thinking.

Thinking like Jesus, but not.

My mind was always wondering, attempting to amaze me.

My mind was on fire.

I had to challenge myself with my own mind.

I was the best at what I did, and no one could do it better.

Thinking like Jesus, but not.

It is easy to strain a brain. Overthinking.

Not knowing which side of your brain to use.

The right or the left.

Thinking like Jesus, but not.

I had to put my mind on pause.

I had lost sight of Jesus.

I had to accept that I could not think like Jesus.

. . . .

DEVILISHLY

I've got devilish ways that make me
misbehave.

I've got an angel on my left shoulder that
comforts me.

I've got a devil on my right shoulder that
misguides me.

I want to play nice with a little sugar and
honey,

But the devil in me always makes me do it.
I'm going to act up on you.

Oh, those devilish ways!

I want to carry the love of God in me,

but oh, those devilish ways always get the
best of me.

Oh, those devilish ways!

You will hear me say it "The Devil made me
do it.

I have misbehaved once again."

I will kick a man when he is down. I will
even bite a baby back.

Oh, those devilish ways!

. . . .

7

I don't want to misbehave, but sometimes,
I can't help myself.

If you see me grinning with a sneaky smile,

don't be fool by that innocent smile.

There is nothing innocent about me.

Oh, those devilish ways!

I may have devilish ways, but I'm just an
innocent angel at heart.

BLINDED

When you think that you have everything,
you can become blind.

Living off your high horse and cannot see.

I was blind and could not see.

It is very easy to forget

Where you came from and where you are
going.

It was me, all me.

I was blind and could not see.

I wanted to step on who I could and walk
on who I could.

I even refused to give a bum some money.

Choosing not to help anyone.

I was blind and could not see.

My head was getting big and bigger.

I got the big head. My head was high in the
sky.

I thought I was winning on Jesus's time.

I was blind and could not see.

Yes, I was living the good life. Rich and all.

I found myself not enjoying myself.

. . . .

I had the Devil in my ear.

Pushing me to do wrong and to mistreat.

I was blind and could not see.

You must learn wherefore your blessings come.

Is it by Jesus?

True blessings come from above.

I was blind and could not see.

To all of those who think they have made it:

Please don't become blind and not see.

Hold on to your blessings. Be humble.

Humble and seeing.

TREACHEROUS HEART

I got burdened down with my own burdens
of this world.

I wanted to be like the Joneses. Living an
extravagant life.

You name it, I did it.

Oh, that treacherous heart of mine.

I was committing sin upon sin.

My pride wouldn't let me be.

I envied and lusted after worldly stuff.

Greed motivated me.

Oh, that treacherous heart of mine.

I had no time for Jesus. It was all about me.

. . . .

Oh, that treacherous heart of mine.

I was a sloth, lazy to movement.

I gorged myself with food and wine.

It was a good life, lacking stamina.

Oh, that treacherous heart of mine.

I was cold. Quick with the wrath of anger.

My words sliced smooth like a butter knife.

Oh, that treacherous heart of mine.

My heart lacks the ability to feel,

Making me lose out on that loving feeling.

Oh, that treacherous heart of mine.

We need to keep treachery out of our hearts.

Make time for Jesus. Stop and enjoy the scenery.

Life is too short for treachery.

Clean hearts have clean souls.

CALLING

I heard my phone ringing. I was too busy to take the call.

Left message: Missed call from Heaven.

I kept going about with my everyday life.

Too busy to check the messages.

Huh, my phone started ringing again.

Not now. Still too busy to take the call.

Left message: Missed call from Heaven.

I start thinking.

"The way this phone is ringing, it must be a bill collector."

Thinking.

. . . .

"The next time this phone starts ringing, I'm going to press decline."

My phone starts flashing. My ringtone changes.

Not tonight. I am still too busy to take the call.

Left message: Missed call from Heaven.

I was playing cat-and-mouse with the calls.

Let me see. How many calls did I miss?

First message: Missed call from Heaven. Second message: Missed call from Heaven. Third message: Missed call from Heaven.

I said, "Oh Lord, I have missed my calls from Heaven."

It was Jesus on the line. Scared but saying, "I've got to call Jesus back."

I returned the call. Got a message. Jesus was unavailable to take the call. Message - I don't want to trouble you Jesus; but I miss your calls.

The next day, my phone start ringing.

I took the call.

It was a call from Heaven with Jesus checking in.

Check on me, Lord. Check on me.

. . . .

Warning

Warning: don't make me go tell Jesus on
you.

I'm going to tell.

You were friendly but unfriendly.

You tried to mistreat me and speak ill of me.

I'm going to tell Jesus on you.

Watch out I am highly favored and blessed
by Jesus. Covered in his blood.

If you mess with me, you mess with him.

Don't make me go tell Jesus on you.

When I tried to do right by you. You tried
to act up on me.

Loving me can't be that hard.

Don't make me go tell Jesus on you.

When I made a move to improve, you tried
to hold me back.

Lying and cheating is your way.

Warning: don't make me go tell Jesus on
you.

You wanted to compete but didn't know
how.

So, you tried to take my integrity.

. . . .

15

Warning: don't make me go tell Jesus on you.

You walked as if you had no conscience.

Smiling and grinning with no smile. Trying to stick a blade in my back.

Don't make me go tell Jesus on you.

Your game is deceit, gathering lost souls in defeat.

But the soul will cry out in defeat.

Making me go tell Jesus on you.

Let this be a warning to you.

I come with backup. Jesus.

Don't make me go tell Jesus on you.

TICKTOCK

Time passes within the second, minutes, and hour.

It moves by seasons: spring, summer, fall, and winter.

But what is true time? His time.

Ticktock, the clock is ticking. Here I come, Jesus. Here I come.

As you move through life, time becomes important.

You must account for your time.

Ticktock, the clock is ticking. Here I come, Jesus. Here I come.

You have present time, past time. Let's not

. . . .

17

forget the time of the future.

It's not what you do but how you do it. Jesus is waiting.

Ticktock, the clock is ticking. Here I come, Jesus. Here I come.

With all of who I am and what I am, I want to thank Jesus for allowing me the time to get it right.

Savor your times with the living because that too shall pass.

Ticktock, the clock is ticking. Here I come, Jesus. Here I come.

How does it end?

It ends with a silent stare and gaze into the eyes of Jesus.

With my hands held tightly by Jesus. Jesus won't let go.

Ticktock, my life has ended. Ticktock, I am with Jesus.

When Jesus extends his hand; please take it.

Ticktock, the clock is ticking. Here I come, Jesus. Here I come.

Ticktock, please don't let your time run out with Jesus.

Let's get it right while we can.

Ticktock, the clock is ticking.

. . . .

PART 2:
Praising

GLORY

It is easy to get caught up in your own hype.

Thinking that you are all that.

Thinking that you are the creator of blessings.

Taking credit for God's glory.

Don't get caught up in claiming God's glory.

All glories go to God.

The God I serve is a jealous God.

Put no other before him.

You can be the vassal, but God is the blood.

Don't get caught up in claiming God's glory.

Give credit to him for the work: but God, but Jesus.

You can be a doctor, but you are not a healer.

You can be a cook, but you are not the chef.

Don't get caught up in claiming God's glory.

We all want to shine.

Put the spotlight on me,

but the glory still goes to God.

. . . .

Don't get caught up in claiming God's glory.

Moses went to the mountaintop,

and God showed him the Promised Land.

Moses got caught claiming God's glory.

Don't get caught up in claiming God's glory.

Don't lose sight of where your blessings
come from.

Give God all the glories.

Don't get caught up in claiming God's glory.

Never downplay God and his work.

Glory to God.

I START PRAYING

Do you know praying works?

It is not what you are praying for.

It is who you are praying to.

I start praying.

How do I pray?

Sometimes, I just lie in my bed.

Praying for a blessing for my family and this world.

I start praying.

Then, there is my drive to work.

I'm taking time out for Jesus.

Thanking him for all my blessings

and asking him for his protection for the day.

I start praying.

One of my friends got sick.

It looked like he wasn't going to make it.

The doctors gave up on him.

I start praying.

"Jesus, I'm in need of a favor.

Jesus, can you tell death to get back?"

. . . .

23

He is still among the living.

I start praying.

When life gets too hard for me,

I go into the closet and take to my knees.

I got to put some work in on this pray. I got to get this one right.

I start praying.

I wanted to be elevated.

I start praying, "Lord, let this be."

It had to be something God could see and wanted for me.

I start praying.

Oh, when I start praying,

there is a blessing coming my way or someone's way.

I'm calling on the names of Jesus and his Father.

My pray just went into overdrive.

I can't let up. Still praying and still down on my knees.

I had to stay down on my knees for you and me.

Bless me and bless you.

Let it come, Jesus. We will receive it.

. . . .

I keep praying. Let it come.

I want you to start praying and keep praying
until the end.

God is going to bless you and me.

I am still praying.

COVER ME

I saw Jesus on the mountaintop.

I made a covenant with Jesus.

His body! His blood! Cover me!

I said, "Jesus, something is coming for me.

Cover me. Don't let go."

The ground started shaking.

Jesus said, "My body! My blood!

Cover thee. No harm shall come to thee!"

There was a trembling in the bush.

The voice said, "Let her come unto me."

The covenant had been made.

The bond could not be broken.

Jesus said, "I stand for thee. I have already died for thee.

This one is mine."

I started looking around. I said, "Jesus is speaking for me."

His body! His blood! Cover me!

It was on that mountaintop

When my covenant was sealed with Jesus.

His body! His blood! Cover me!

. . . .

27

LIFE VINE

Do you want to live forever?

There is only one way in: by Jesus.

Jesus is the true vine to everlasting life.

Hold on to the vine.

Once, I was saved but became a backslider.

Taking my eyes off the prize.

Hold on to the vine.

I took Jesus for granted.

Thinking he would always be there for me.

Hold on to the vine.

I was a child at play on the Devil's stomping grounds.

He bewildered me.

Showing me all that could be mine within a blink of an eye.

Hold on to the vine.

With life, you must make sacrifices sometimes.

Nothing comes easy or cheap.

What will you sacrifice?

Hold on to the vine.

. . . .

I already knew my answer.

I would give up everything for the vine.

Hold on to the vine.

Jesus's vine doesn't need water.

It is everlasting.

Hold on to the vine.

ABOUT JESUS

It is all about Jesus.

I want to introduce you to a man named
Jesus who became my savior.

Yes, it is all about Jesus.

He is a loving son who showed compassion
to me.

No greater love could be shown because he
gave his own life for me.

Yes, it is all about Jesus.

He is a miracle worker who is seated at the
foot of the throne.

Yes, he is that man. The man who my heart
longed for.

. . . .

Yes, it is all about Jesus.

I can't help but love the man. I love calling his name. Jesus, Jesus.

He is my all in all. He is my everything. He is that man.

Yes, it is all about Jesus.

In his name, the impossible is possible.

He can make the weak strong and give hope to all.

Yes, it is all about Jesus.

It is the calmness in his voice when he speaks my name.

It is the way he can soothe my soul.

Yes, it is all about Jesus.

It is the gratification of life in paradise that this man is offering.

No more sickness, no aging. Life itself with the ability to live forever.

Yes, it is all about Jesus.

Once again, I proudly want to introduce you to this man named Jesus.

The one and only Jesus Christ. My savior, your savior, Jesus.

Yes, it is all about Jesus.

. . . .

I Needed Jesus

Jesus is the overseer in my life.

If he must chastise me, he will.

Every, child needs discipling, every now and then.

I needed Jesus.

I am just a sucker for his love.

I moon after him. I love following in his footsteps.

Jesus always encourages me to follow.

I needed Jesus.

When I am with Jesus, my mind is at peace.

I let him do all the worrying for me.

I needed Jesus.

If it looks like I may stumble and fall,

His hands are always there to catch and embrace me.

I shall not fall.

I needed Jesus.

I am like a kid in a candy store when I am with Jesus.

I just don't know how to control myself.

. . . .

There are so many questions to ask.

I needed Jesus.

If you feel the need that you need Jesus,

Try following in his footsteps.

I needed Jesus.

THE CLIMB

I was at the bottom of the mountain.

Something was beckoning me to climb to
the top.

I started following the fiery light.

My eyes were narrowing and looking up.

I got God in my sight.

I was being summoned to his greatness.

I was scared to climb that mountain.

It was smoking at the top.

I got God in my sight.

His voice sounded like thunder,

Sending chills through my body.

God told me that he was the one, God
Almighty, himself.

ask of him what I want.

I got God in my sight.

Do you know what type of feeling you get

When God is willing to speak to you?

That feeling was unknown to me.

I said, "I must be dead and have made it to
Heaven."

. . . .

I've got God in my sight.

I asked, "Are you willing to give me anything?"

God said to me, "I am the God of all things. I make all things possible, including life."

I've got God in my sight.

I asked myself, "What would I ask?"

The answer became clear to me.

I asked, "God for himself."

There is nothing greater than God.

God told me that I had been summoned and that the sentence would be life itself.

I had God in my sight.

I've been to the mountaintop.

And at the top, I met God as a burning bush.

The bush burned so bright.

I could not lay my eyes upon on him.

I had God in my sight.

. . . .

BUT GOD

If it wasn't for God,

There would be no sun and moon in the sky.

Isn't God good?

When all was lost,

God gave up his own son.

Isn't God good?

When the Devil made me cry,

God sent an angel to dry my eyes.

Isn't God good?

When I was a lost lamb,

God sent Jesus to me.

Isn't God good?

When I need a blessing,

God always comes through for me.

Isn't God good?

When I needed a testimony,

God gave me a test.

Isn't God good?

When my faith fell short,

God strengthened me.

· · · · · · · · · ·

Isn't God good?

When God spoke to me,

he uplifted me.

Isn't God good?

The goodness of God is great.

Isn't God good?

MY ALL

Ask yourself, "What is holding me to this world?

Can I give it all up to follow Jesus?"

I'm giving Jesus my all.

Don't get me wrong: all people love material things.

With some, it makes them who they are.

It defines them.

For me, I'm going to give it all to Jesus.

I'm giving Jesus my all.

You cannot live with regrets by choosing Jesus.

As I always say, "I won't look back."

I feel no self-pity by choosing to follow Jesus.

I'm giving Jesus my all.

If you are trying to choose Jesus

because of riches and fame,

you are choosing him for all the wrong reasons.

What is your reason?

I'm giving Jesus my all.

. . . .

You can't play both sides with Jesus.

In the morning when you rise, you are saved.

By the end of the day, you are unsaved.

I'm giving Jesus my all.

I rise because of Jesus.

I live because of Jesus.

I am because of Jesus.

I love because of Jesus.

I'm giving Jesus my all.

When I rise, I thank Jesus for paving the way.

I'm giving Jesus my all.

PART 3:
Uplifting

CREEPING WITH JESUS

I went creeping with Jesus.

Jesus will go to some low places to find a lost soul.

Jesus said, "We have to be able to go where I am needed."

I went creeping with Jesus.

I found myself at the jailhouse.

I showed my badge with the name Worker for Jesus.

I told the jailer, "A lost soul is here, crying out for Jesus."

Soul saved. I went creeping with Jesus.

We were walking past a nightclub.

Jesus said, "Someone in there is calling my name."

We had to go in. Found an unsaved soul in that building.

Soul saved. I went creeping with Jesus.

There are all kind of souls in hospitals.

I said, "Jesus, there are maybe too many for us to save."

Jesus said, "No soul left behind."

. . . .

Soul saved. I went creeping with Jesus.

We even went into the churches.

There were lost souls everywhere, crying out for Jesus.

Jesus said, "These souls need saving. I am the savior of souls."

Soul saved. I went creeping with Jesus.

Something kept calling us forward.

I said, "Jesus, where is that lost soul?"

Jesus said, "There is a soul stuck between Heaven and Earth."

I said, "Jesus, how are we going to get there?"

Jesus said, "We are going to ascend, and we won't need any wings."

Soul saved. I went creeping with Jesus.

Jesus is a soul savior no matter where that soul may be.

I want to thank Jesus for saving all souls like yours and mine.

I'm going creeping with Jesus.

· · · · · · · · · ·

The Name of My Father

Yes, I had an earthly father

who I called my daddy, father, and
sometimes Chester.

Calling my father by his name.

Some children never get to know their
fathers or their names.

Missing out on a blessing.

All children should know their fathers.

Calling my father by his name.

I have three sons who know their father very
well.

He answers to Pop and even Pugh.

No matter what they call him, when they
call, he's going to answer.

He is one of the good fathers. Too short and
too few.

Calling my father by his name.

I want to take you to the next level.

Did you know Jesus has a Father, who is our
Heavenly Father?

Yes, I did.

. . . .

Calling my father by his name.

I'm getting a little excited, now.

Because I'm getting ready to talk about my
Heavenly Father.

Calling my father by his name.

What names do I call him?

First, there is God, my Father.

I feel very intimate with that one that lets
me know I am his child.

Second, there is Almighty God.

That one tells me my father has all the
power.

Third, there is the Lord.

That tells me he has mercy for me.

Fourth, let me tell you about the best name
that some don't even know.

I am getting ready to get personal with my
father.

I am going to call him by his real name,
Jehovah.

It is a name above all names. The best name
ever.

When I say it, something swells up inside of
me.

Jehovah, the creator of all life, is your

. . . .

Heavenly Father's **name.**

I want to call my father by his name.
Jehovah is his name.

TESTIMONY

I want to testify.

As we live life, everyone gets a testimony

Because the journey isn't easy.

It is about the test, a test.

I want to testify.

Some of my tests were small but meaningful.

It was the hard test, the big test, that made
me worry.

I want to testify.

First test: I had to learn who Jesus was.

That, I passed. I learned who he was. I know
him.

I want to testify.

Second test: Can I put Jesus first?

That, I passed. I had to put myself aside and
put Jesus on the forefront.

I had to turn my life over to Jesus.

I want to testify.

Third test was a whopper. The Devil tried
me.

Tried to make me turn against Jesus.

. . . .

Tried to get me to get on his team.

I am proud to say, that too, I passed.

I want to testify.

Fourth test: Can I keep my eyes on Jesus?

I had to be strong and devoted to pass this test.

All kind of troubles came my way, tempting me to cuss Jesus.

I said, "I was an A student and a loyal student. I'm fast learner."

I was shaken but passing.

I want to testify.

Fifth test: Can I tell you how good God's been to me? Sounds easy but hard. I got to sell the Almighty to you. I got to make a believer out of you.

Can I lead you to Jesus and his Father? That too, I pass.

I want to testify.

I can't get it all in, in this poem,

But next time, I will tell you a little bit more.

I want to testify.

. . . .

49

FRIENDLESS

I was a private person.

I was lonely and had no friends.

Because I didn't have any friends, I had no one to talk to.

I started talking to myself.

I was friendless and lonely.

I was too mean and hateful to socialize.

Saying, "I don't need nobody. I can play with myself."

I was friendless and lonely.

One day, I was on my way to church.

I heard an old hymn playing on the radio. "You got a friend in Jesus."

I was friendless and lonely.

Do you know that old saying? Everybody needs a friend.

I said, "I'm going to find myself a friend, and it may be with Jesus."

I was friendless and lonely.

Instead of talking to myself, I started talking to Jesus.

Did you know Jesus was listening?

. . . .

I was friendless and lonely.

Not only did I find a friend in Jesus—we bonded, and a friendship began.

Not lonely. Got a friend.

As of today, Jesus may not be my only friend, but Jesus is my best friend.

He is the type of friend who you just can't keep to yourself.

As my grandbabies are always saying, "You got to share."

Therefore, I am sharing this with you. Try Jesus as a friend.

Let Jesus be your best friend. There is enough of him to go around.

Please Don't be Friendless and Lonely!

. . . .

LET'S GET HYPE

I woke up this morning with a smile on my face.

God has woken me with the breath of life once again.

I'm ready to get hype.

I know Jesus will be my shield and protection against all foes

no matter the shape of form.

I'm ready to get hype.

I know the creator of life. All my blessings come from God.

He provides for all my needs. Today will be a good day.

I'm ready to get hype.

I get fired up when I talk about Jesus.

I am on the hunt, looking for followers.

I am going in with his words.

I'm ready to get hype.

I'm ready to let the world know that I am a believer in Jesus.

I'm ready to get hype.

If you are ready to get hype with Jesus,

. . . .

You'd better take a deep breath and exhale.

Jesus will be in charge today.

Where he leads, we are going to follow.

We're ready to get hype.

We're going to clap our hands, stomp our feet, and bob our heads.

Let's get hype!

. . . .

DEBT PAID IN FULL

There was a price to pay for our sins. Man couldn't pay it.

Even the angels in Heaven couldn't pay for our sins.

It had to be Jesus. Debt paid in full.

Jesus asked his Father

what price he had to pay for the people's sins.

God said, "With your life, my son."

It had to be Jesus. Debt paid in full.

Jesus said to his Father, "I am willing to pay the price.

I will sacrifice and give my own life up for their sins."

It had to be Jesus. Debt paid in full.

God so loved this world. The love was brighter than the sun in the sky. It glistened like a star. The price would be paid with his son's life.

It had to be Jesus. Debt paid in full.

When you think about the price Jesus paid for you and me,

It is astonishing and amazing. It was the

. . . .

54

courage and the heart
for the love of the people.
It had to be Jesus. Debt paid in full.
It was my Jesus, your Jesus, our Jesus
who paid the debt for you and me?
He died upon the cross.
It had to be Jesus. Debt paid in full.

SPOKEN WORDS

I heard a voice speaking to me.

It sounded like a sweet melody.

I heard Jesus speak.

The voice was saying, "Come, come to me.
Come to me, your Savior."

I heard Jesus speak.

I got spooked. I asked myself, "Did you hear
that?"

My flesh started tingling. I perked up.

I heard Jesus speak.

I said, "This could be a broken record

Constantly playing my song."

Oh, the music sounds so good to me.

I heard Jesus speak.

I said, "Yes Lord, yes Lord, I hear you. I
shall obey."

I said, "What is it that you want with me?"

Jesus said, "Come, come unto me."

I heard Jesus speak.

With me being me, I said, "What did you
say, Jesus?"

. . . .

The melody replayed itself. "Come, come to me."

I heard Jesus speak. I heard Jesus speak.

I said, "Speak it to me, Jesus. In my soul and in my spirit."

I heard Jesus speak.

Did you hear Jesus speak?

If you can hear Jesus speak,

Stand up, raise your hand.

Speak these words:

I heard Jesus speak.

. . . .

FOUND

I was a fool and a sinner. Nothing mattered to me.

I was living life to its fullest.

Carefree. Let me be.

A change came over me.

Jesus took a hold of me. I was found but not lost.

Jesus was residing in me.

That which was within shone through.

The light of Jesus was shining out of me.

Jesus was residing in me.

I had a glow about me.

My heart became heavy. I was bursting with joy.

Jesus was residing in me.

He made me feel what I did not want to feel.

Jesus was in place and in play.

Jesus was residing in me.

I said, "My heart, my flesh. Can this be?"

Jesus was residing in me.

. . . .

I had the same heart but a changed heart.

He who lives within.

Jesus was residing in me.

Can you let Jesus find you and change you?

Jesus wants to reside in you.

THE TOUCH

Oh, the things that Jesus can do with a
simple touch.

It's mind blowing. It's electrifying.

Touch me, Jesus. Touch me.

Sometimes, when I get worried, I need to be
held.

I need to be comforted by the Lord.

I want Jesus to put his hands on me.

Touch me, Jesus. Touch me.

With his touch, my heart starts beating fast.

I get all pumped up. I can't hold back the
excitement.

Jesus got his hands on me.

Touch me, Jesus. Touch me.

It came as a breeze of wind. Oh, the Holy
Ghost was upon me.

Touch me, Jesus. Touch me.

I said, "Get back; give me room." I rose.
Stood straight up on my feet. My feet got
light. I was gliding across the floor.

Jesus had his hand on me.

Touch me, Jesus. Touch me.

. . . .

The next time you are in need,

A simple touch from Jesus can fix all your needs.

Touch me, Jesus. Touch me.

WORK ON ME

I was trying to get it right. It was years in the making.

God was working on me. Work on me, Lord. Work on me.

I wanted to be a child of God. Jesus paid the price. His blood saved me.

Work on me, Lord. Work on me.

If Jesus can pay the price with his life,

Surely, I can pay the price with my soul.

Work on me, Lord. Work on me.

I was stripped down to my bare bones. Getting ready to pay the price.

God was working on me. Work on me, Lord. Work on me.

I was all in. I was being rebuilt. I can't stop. I got pushed forward because God was working on me. Work on me, Lord. Work on me.

He consumes me. He fills me.

God is working on me. Work on me, Lord. Work on me.

When the work was done, I saw the light.

Jesus stepped in and resided within me.

. . . .

Work on me, Lord. Work on me.

If the time has come for you to turn your
life over to God,

Believe it. Shout it.

Work on me, Lord. Work on me.

. . . .

STILLNESS

The stillness of my soul.

My soul and spirit were in an uproar.

The Devil kept bothering me.

God stilled my soul.

The Devil is fighting a losing battle

and is coming for all our souls.

Put all of you and your trust in God.

God stilled my soul.

The Devil is known to harass.

He won't let up.

You got to pray hard to get him off you.

God stilled my soul.

You got to know when the Devil is at work.

He is dishing out false dreams and hope.

Don't be fooled.

God stilled my soul.

Salvation is a full-time job.

You are always on the clock.

Don't break the chain; each link is
connected.

God stilled my soul.

. . . .

I will leave you with this:

When the soul is in an uproar,

It takes God to still the soul.

May your soul be calm and at peace.

I SAW

Ever since I was a child my grandmother
told me

that I was special born with the gift of sight.

I saw.

Every child did not have it only a selected
few.

The gift to see the unseen.

I saw.

I saw the coming of the Lord.

The bible said that Jesus shall return.

I saw.

Heaven open.

The Angels stood at attention surrounding
the world.

I saw.

Time stood still.

The great chariot was approaching carrying

King Jesus.

The clouds lightened and darkened at the
same time.

I saw.

. . . .

Jesus raced around the world

at the speed of light.

For all to see

to bear witness to his greatness.

I saw.

The dead flowers start reblooming.

Even the grave was giving up it dead.

Can you imagine seeing the return of Jesus?

Coming back to reclaim what is his.

I saw.

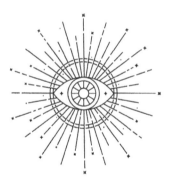

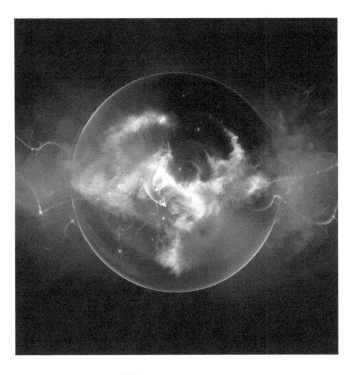

PART 4:
Motivating

By Chance

I was at my last end. Didn't want to give up. Betting on life itself.

I took a chance with Jesus.

Bet in. Let it roll. I'm betting on Jesus for the win.

I tried to hold out to the bitter end. Life was passing me by.

I needed a win.

Bet in. Let it roll. I'm betting on Jesus for the win.

I can't be scared. I've got to put my trust in Jesus.

Bet in. Let it ride. I'm betting on Jesus for the win.

My health was failing me. These bills were piling high.

I've got to chance it with Jesus.

Bet in. Let it roll. I'm betting on Jesus for the win.

Everything else had failed me. Even the Devil tried to play me. Losing was not an option.

I decided I was going to chance it with

. . . .

Jesus.

Bet in. Let it roll. I'm betting on Jesus for the win.

My hands started itching. My eye was jumping.

Bet in. Let it roll. I'm betting on Jesus for the win.

Never be scared to bet on Jesus for the win.

PICK ME UP

A cry went up, but a blessing came down.

Hallelujah, amen. Pick me up, Jesus. Pick me up.

My sorrows ran deep.

Pick me up, Jesus. Pick me up.

I was broken, but God uplifted me.

Hallelujah, amen. Pick me up, Jesus. Pick me up.

I lost my voice, couldn't even cry, but I found my way.

Pick me up, Jesus. Pick me up.

I was wounded but not dead.

Hallelujah, amen. Pick me up, Jesus. Pick me up.

It was my pain, my hurts, but Jesus saw me through it.

Hallelujah, amen. Pick me up, Jesus. Pick me up.

All my praises and all my glories go to the man upstairs.

Hallelujah, amen. Pick me up, Jesus. Pick me up.

. . . .

Did you know that Jesus will carry you in your hour of need?

Hallelujah, amen. Pick me up, Jesus. Pick me up.

God said, "Woe to the earth." Let's not forget

When a cry goes up, blessings come down.

Hallelujah, amen. Pick me up, Jesus. Pick me up.

Bless the reader and receiver of these words.

May your blessings be great.

Hallelujah, amen. Pick me up, Jesus. Pick me up.

I Want a Ride

Have you ever been stranded with no ride?

I want to enlighten you about a ride I
caught with Jesus

By humming these words:

I want to ride with Jesus. Can I ride?

Smelling good, all dressed up and ready to go.

Little did I know, my ride wasn't ready.

Thinking, "What's wrong with this ride, and
where am I going?"

Within a flash, I heard these words:

No charge. No fare. Get on board.

I started smiling and humming:

I want to ride with Jesus. Can I ride?

The train was filling up fast. I needed room
to get on board.

Thinking to myself, "People, make room. I
need to get on board."

A bright path opened when they heard me hum:

I want to ride with Jesus. Can I ride?

I heard the wheels start chucking and the
whistle blowing.

The angels were making last call, all aboard.

. . . .

I took my seat. Humming,

I want to ride with Jesus. Can I ride?

I looked forward, and Jesus was at the
wheel.

All where I had been flashed before me.

Jesus turned and said, "Buckle up, this train
is rolling."

Once again, I was smiling and humming:

I want to ride with Jesus. Can I ride?

You may not know where you are going, but
you know where you've been.

With Jesus, you can't go anywhere but up.

Are you ready? Let's ride. Let's hum this
together:

I want to ride with Jesus. Can I ride?

I Can't Fall

I can't fall because I've been elevated to
ascend higher.

Take me higher, Lord. Take me high.

Life is hard. The times and world we are
living in try to hold you down and keep you
back. My rebuttal is, "I'm going high."

Take me higher, Lord. Take me high.

I am always looking upward. Someone is
calling my name. I find myself saying,

"Jesus, I want to go high. Where you lead, I
will follow."

Take me higher, Lord. Take me high.

My feet start wriggling. My body gets light.

I am floating upward, sailing in the sky.

Higher, Lord. Take me high.

My soul, my body, and my mind are free to
fly with Jesus.

I can't fall because I chose to ascend upward
with Jesus.

Take me higher, Lord. Take me high.

Just for one moment in time, can you let
yourself be free and fly with Jesus?

. . . .

I can hear you saying,

Take me higher, Lord. Take me high.

Flying with Jesus is the best high and the
only high you will ever need. It consoles
you. It will amaze you.

Take me higher, Lord. Take me high.

I can't fall. Take me higher, Lord.
Take me high.

. . . .

I AM ON MY WAY

Somewhere along my way, I lost my way,

But I stand before you today

Proud, covered in the blood of Jesus.

Yes, Lord, I am on my way.

When I hit rock bottom, there was nothing
beneath me

that my heart could desire, so I looked
upward.

What did I see?

Yes, Lord, all the glories of God. King Jesus
himself.

Yes, Lord, I am on my way.

. . . .

79

Sometimes in this old life,
you get knocked down,

But remember you will rise; you shall rise.

Stand tall in your devotion to God.

Yes, Lord, I am on my way.

With my heart in my hands and confusion
on my brain,

My burdens weight heavy on me.

Yes, Lord, I am on my way.

I stand in the shadow of greatness. Uplifted
by the wings of Jesus.

Yes, Lord, I am on my way.

In these days and hours, Jesus is still looking
for followers.

If you can stand for Jesus, let me hear you
say,

Yes, Lord, I am on my way.

LEVEL UP

Have you ever had that feeling?

when something just comes over you

and you just can't shake it?

Level up! We are going up!

You know that you know

that God's going to work a miracle for you.

Yes, he will.

Level up! We are going up!

I will stomp out anything that tries to get in
my way.

Said it like you mean it: "I'm leveling up!"

I see stars in my eyes.

Level up! We are going up!

There is no doubt

That Jesus is going to make a way.

I am fully charged up.

I can smell the success of victory.

Level up! We are going up!

By now, I know you are all fired up and
ready to go.

We are leveling up!

. . . .

Fingers up.

Level up! We are going up!

PART 5:
Inspiring

The Uplift

People are always trying to get in my way.

Trying to steal and block my blessings.

Learn this: you can't bring someone down
who God has lifted.

The uplift. There is no way but up.

Everyone is always thinking, why her and
not me?

Maybe it is not your time yet for an
uplifting.

Stop trying to bring me down.

The uplift. There is no way but up.

Do you know that your family will get
jealous and envy you?

Wishing the worst for you.

Stop trying to bring me down.

The uplift. There is no way but up.

My man was supposed to uplift me.

Holding me higher than all others.

I was thinking, true, but not true.

Stop trying to bring me down.

The uplift. There is no way but up.

. . . .

Then, there is someone always saying

"Are you afraid that someone else is going to get your blessing?"

No, I'm not.

What is mended for you or given to you by God is yours,

And I always claim my prize.

Stop trying to bring me down.

The uplift. There is no way but up.

I've been uplifted by God, and no one is going to bring me down.

The uplift. There is no way but up.

MISSING ANGEL

Heaven is such a beautiful place.

I know the streets are paved with gold.

There is a missing angel in heaven.

Heaven awaits me.

Heaven is always busy.

Some of the new angels have already taken
their seats.

I had a new angel trying to babysit me.

Baby angel's gone missing.

Heaven awaits me.

I had broken my wing and could not fly.

God made roll call.

God said, "I know my count was right; one of
my children is missing." Heaven awaits me.

I got nervous and scared,

Thinking my father was going to be mad at me.

Who wants a child with one wing?

Heaven awaits me.

God said, "Jesus, you go looking."

Jesus said, "I will not return without the
child angel."

. . . .

87

Heaven awaits me.

I heard Jesus calling my name.

He said, "Don't make me call your number."

I called out to Jesus, saying,

"I am disfigured and cannot fly. I have broken one of my wings.

I don't want you to abandon me."

Jesus came to me and laid his hands on my broken wing.

He said, "You are all better now; my father been calling your name.

Heaven is awaiting you."

Child angel found, no longer missing. I'm an angel in Heaven.

FAITH

Can you believe in something that you cannot, see?

Can you trust in someone you cannot, see?

For a second, I want to help you with your faith.

Bonded by my faith.

My grandmother taught it to my mother.

My mother taught it to me.

Hold on to your faith.

Little money or no money,

But living on faith, that God's going to make everything okay.

Bonded by my faith.

My faith was rooted in me. It is always with me.

I have the faith to believe God is real. Unseen in the flesh but real.

Bonded by my faith.

My faith inspires me. It guides me.

It pushes me forward when I want to stand still.

It picks me up when I want to lie down.

. . . .

Bonded by my faith.

My faith is so strong in Jesus

That I will not question any of his actions.

I know Jesus will do right by me.

Bonded by my faith.

I know it is hard for a person to believe in something unseen.

Try closing your eyes and clearing your mind.

Look around you and see all of God's glories.

Bonded by my faith.

I've got to believe in something.

I'd rather believe in Jesus instead of believing in nothing.

Bonded by my faith.

READY

I started a conversation with Jesus

With an invitation of him living inside of
me.

I wasn't ready yet. I was not worthy.

Not ready, unworthy.

I said, "Jesus, I am not offended by thee."

I'm not ready; but I am getting ready.

Not ready, unworthy.

It takes time to prepare your body and your
mind for Jesus.

This is not an overnight process. I was in it
for the long haul.

Not ready, unworthy.

I had to be steady and consistent.

You must be worthy for Jesus

To step in and invade your body and mind.

Not ready, unworthy.

There was a purification of my body and
mind.

The preparation was on its way. I got to
become worthy.

Not ready, unworthy.

. . . .

I held fast and wouldn't give up. I put all my
trust in Jesus.

An explosion was taking place in me.

Still not ready. Still not worthy.

Not ready, unworthy.

By the end of the journey. I became ready
and worthy.

Invitation accepted.

The invasion of my body and mind by Jesus
has just begun.

I was ready and worthy.

HEAVENLY CHOICE

Can you choose between right and wrong?

My mind was playing tricks on me.

Which will it be: choice one or choice two,
Heaven or Hell?

It is easy to make a wrong turn in life.

I can go forward, or I can go backward.

I can turn to the left or turn to the right.

Which will it be: choice one or choice two,
Heaven or Hell?

I was led astray. Made a wrong turn at that
turn.

Oh no, I was on my way to Hell. Bad
choice. Wrong way.

Let me back up. I got to get back on the
right path.

Which will it be: choice one or choice two,
Heaven or Hell?

I am back on my way.

On the road to Heaven. Right choice. Right
way.

Little did I know, there were speed bumps
on this road.

. . . .

Which will it be: choice one or choice two,
Heaven or Hell?

I got caught speeding by an angel.

I said, "My record is clean." He said, "Is it
now?"

Made me start thinking, what had I done?

The angel said, "Clean record, no work."

Which will it be: choice one or choice two,
Heaven or Hell?

You can make the right choice; but you
must put in the work.

I wanted a record with God.

I need God to remember my name on
Judgment Day.

My choice was choice one, Heaven. Made a
record for Judgment Day.

KNOCK! KNOCK!

It was in the midnight hour. I heard a knock
at my door.

I looked around and thought. Who could be
knocking at my door?

Knock! Knock! It was Jesus at my door.

I opened my door because I recognized
Jesus.

I said, "Jesus, you are looking cold and
hungry.

My home is your home. Let me feed you."

Knock! Knock! It was Jesus at my door.

Jesus sat down at my table.

I said, "Jesus, where are you going, and can I
go with you?"

Jesus said, "Yes, my child, you can follow.

If you get weary and can't keep up, I will
carry you."

Knock! Knock! It was Jesus at my door.

I said, "Jesus, my load is light. I have no
baggage.

I'm going with you, as is."

Jesus, I am down with you. Jesus, I am

. . . .

95

going to follow you."

Knock! Knock! It was Jesus at my door.

I said, "Jesus, it is troubles in those streets.

Let me cover you with this cloak."

Jesus said, "I've got to be seen. Let's sit, eat, and be merry.

The time is near."

Knock! Knock! It was Jesus at my door.

When Jesus comes a knocking open your door.

Knock! Knock! It was Jesus at my door.

THE HOOK UP

I got the hook with Jesus.

I'm tapping in. Let me in, Jesus. Let me in.

Lord, I am trying to make it to Heaven.

Let me in, Jesus. Let me in.

The Devil tried to restrain me. I need to break these chains.

He's trying to hold me back. Enticing me with the glamorous life.

Lord, I need help to break these chains.

Let me in, Jesus. Let me in.

I had to team up with Jesus to break the chains.

I told Jesus, I'm checking in. Move, Jesus. Let me in.

Jesus, you throw the line, and I will reel them in.

I'm tapping in. Let me in, Jesus. Let me in.

The water got rough. I took the bow.

Jesus goaded the storm. Jesus was tapping in.

What could I do but let him in? I could hardly believe my own eyes. There, Jesus

. . . .

was walking on the water. All peaceful and sound.

Tap in, Jesus. Tap in.

The ship took to land. It was out of sight.

I was overcome. Jesus was ascending to the heavens.

Jesus said, "Look out below; these gates are opening. Come on up."

My feet started tapping. I was dancing.

I was getting into Heaven.

You, too, can get into Heaven by tapping in with Jesus.

I GOT THE HOOKUP WITH JESUS.

.

DESTINY

For a time, I lost me. Giving others power
and control over me.

Giving them the false hope that they were in
control of my destiny.

I'm taking it back. My power.

Stepping and walking all over me.

Giving little or no care to my emotions.

My heart bleeds. My heart feels. Had me an
emotional mess.

I'm taking it back. My power.

I was made to feel that I were nothing and
that love wouldn't come my way.

Belittled and criticized.

I'm taking it back. My power.

I've been stomped on. Battled and bruised.

Scarred mentally and physically. With
someone telling me I wasn't worthy.

Trying to hold me back from my destiny.

I'm taking it back. My power.

I was looking for a way out. Even
considering taking my own life.

. . . .

I started crying to God, and he whistled
these words to me:

"What are you crying for? Take back your
power

because I control your destiny."

I had to lie back and pat my own chest.
Saying, be still my heart.

His words had to resonate in me. I said, no
more.

I am taking back my power because God
controls my destiny.

I believed it, and I live by it.

I took back my power because God controls
my destiny.

Whatever God has in store for you, it is
yours take it.

It is by your choice alone if you let God
control your destiny.

With God in control, you cannot fail.

CALLING ALL WARRIORS

I heard the trumpet blowing, calling all warriors.

Warrior, warrior rises. Warrior, warrior stands tall. Warrior, warrior holds fast.

I looked to my left, and what did I see?

All the heavenly angels standing beside me.

I looked to my right, and there was Jesus Christ himself standing beside me.

It all came clear when I looked above.

It was God Almighty seated at the throne with his voice roaring:

Warrior, warrior rises. Warrior, warrior stands tall. Warrior, warrior holds fast.

It was the power of his voice that stilled me. It strengthened me.

I was ready to battle. Nothing could hold me back.

We started marching. The movement was on.

Warriors, warriors, we rise. Warriors, warriors, we stand. Warriors, warriors, we hold.

. . . .

When you are battling for God, you can't wobble. You've got to hold fast.

I took a blow from life. It wobbled me. I was down but not out.

Once again, I heard the trumpet, calling for all warriors.

Warrior, warrior rises. Warrior, warrior stands tall. Warrior, warrior holds fast.

My back got straight. I was standing tall. I was ready to hold. I am a warrior for the Lord. When he calls, I will answer. I will march forward and hold the line. If need be, I will carry the fallen.

Warrior, warrior, I rose. Warrior, warrior, I stood. Warrior, warrior, I held.

Warriors, you must armor up for battle. Stand in your convictions with God. Let Jesus lead. Can you handle the warrior's call?

Warrior, warrior rises. Warrior, warrior stands tall. Warrior, warrior holds fast.

SMILING

I looked up toward Heaven.

There were God smiling down at me.

Smiling with a purpose.

It surprised me that God could see me.

His piercing eyes pierced my soul.

Smiling with a purpose.

It was a meeting of the minds.

I could see his vision for me.

God's purpose for me.

Smiling with a purpose.

I was being shown all my worth.

I was a part of God's plan.

Isn't that something?

Smiling with a purpose.

His smile lit up the sky.

The tinkles in his eyes had to be stars.

I knew just for a moment in time. I had
made God happy.

Smiling with a purpose.

I started smiling back.

I knew God was reading my mind.

. . . .

I thought whatever you want. I will do my best.

I was smiling with a purpose.

If by chance you look up and see God smiling at you.

Please smile back because God has a purpose for your life.

Smiling with a purpose.

PARADISE

I dream of a better world.

Where there are no more aging, sickness or dying.

Would that be paradise?

Heaven has a number, but this world has no number.

There are people as far as the eyes can see.

Would that be paradise?

There will be no more crying.

I wouldn't be hungry.

Happiness is the reality.

Would that be paradise?

Jesus is preparing a place

call paradise for you and me here on earth.

Do you want to see paradise?

To see paradise, you must choose Jesus.

Jesus is the way.

Could that be paradise?

If I can't make it to heaven

than I will choose happiness here on earth.

I will live forever in paradise. It earthy, but paradise.

. . . .

Jesus will still be King on his heavenly throne.

Jesus has remembered me.

Weary and Shaken

There was a time in my life.

When I tried to carry the weight of the
world

on my shoulders.

I was weary and shaken.

Even the sun in the sky would not shine on
me.

I was at my lowest point in life.

I was weary and shaken.

My brain was spinning out of control.

Not only was I mad at the world.

I was mad at myself.

I was weary and shaken.

I knew not who or where to turn to.

I was lost within myself.

I was weary and shaken.

I had lost all my desire to live.

That when I started crying to Jesus.

Jesus, I need you. Jesus, I need a healing.

Jesus, can you look my way?

I was weary and shaken.

. . . .

Jesus heard my cries and glanced my way.

With that glance, I had a new meaning for my life.

Life was stirring within me.

Life is always the choice with Jesus.

Jesus wanted me to live.

I wanted to live.

I was no longer weary or shaken.

I chose to live life to its fullest.

Unwearied and unshaken

PART 6:
Loving

No Love

It is hard to love someone who chooses not to love you back.

You can't make anyone love you,

but you can buy loving.

I went looking for love.

You can't buy love, but you can buy loving.

I wore my heart on my sleeves.

My love was on display for all to see.

You can't buy love, but you can buy loving.

When someone knows how strong you love them,

They will put your heart in the palm of their hands

and squeeze it at will.

Your love means nothing to them.

They will break your heart as they please.

You can't buy love, but you can buy loving.

If you go down the path of falling in love,

you better learn who you are falling in love with.

Because no love is guaranteed.

. . . .

You can't buy love, but you can buy loving.

Don't go looking for love in all the wrong places.

Sometimes, you must let love find you

Instead of you finding love.

You can't buy love, but you can buy loving.

Let this be a lesson to all.

You can't buy love, but you can buy loving.

BUILT UP

I was built up but let down.

Ladies and gentlemen, I want to talk about

being built up and getting let down.

Love can only take you so far.

Built up and let down.

I had an impeccable love for a man. The sun
rose with him.

He built me up as if I was the only one.

I was his queen, so I believed.

How many queens did he have?

Built up and let down.

This playing field isn't just for the men.

Ladies, you can play dirty too.

You have one man coming through the front
door

while another man is leaving by the back
door.

Built up and let down.

I'm getting ready to knock the ball out of
the ballpark.

False prophecy, everywhere you look.

. . . .

I got a prophet over here and a prophet over there.

Who are these people?

Talking about God got his hands on them.

I'm checking for fingerprints and the palm.

Built up and let down.

People, stop listening to promises made by earthly souls.

You must stand on God's words. His words are everlasting.

The same today as they were yesterday.

Built up and held up.

Jesus can build you up and won't let you down.

His promises are never broken.

I want to be built up and not let down.

I'm starting with my true love, Jesus Christ.

I won't be let down.

WRONG

I love me and my family.

Am I wrong?

I love helping and standing by my friends.

Am I wrong?

I am strong and vulnerable.

Am I wrong?

I love reading and writing.

Am I wrong?

I love challenging myself.

Am I wrong?

I love achieving all my goals.

Am I wrong?

I love life.

Am I wrong?

I love Jesus and his Father.

Am I wrong?

I am blessed and favored by God.

Am I wrong?

The pleasure of love is never wrong.

Am I wrong?

. . . .

What's wrong is being afraid to be wrong.

Everybody carries the burden of being wrong every now and then.

Am I wrong?

Broken

Love is a wonderful feeling.

Everyone should experience love at least
once in a lifetime.

It was the aftermath of love that broke me.

The pain ricocheted through my body.

I was broken.

There was an abomination taking place
upon my heart.

In love, but out of love.

I was broken.

I had to shield my own heart.

The pain was unbearable.

. . . .

Can this heart of mine love again? Too
scared to love.

I was broken.

People were whistling behind my back.

Laughing in my face. Not caring how I felt.

I was broken.

My heart was cracked and bruised,

Stopping my blood from flowing through
my body.

I was broken.

You must counter love with love.

If you love someone and they can't love you
back,

Set them free, and let true love come your
way.

I was broken.

A scarred heart can be healed.

A broken heart can be fixed.

I was in love again.

Temptation

Someone tried to lead me into temptation.

Temptation wasn't for me.

Go away. I won't stray.

Temptation had flesh like gold. A body of a god.

Piercing eyes with a beautiful smile.

Temptation is always pleasing to the eye.

Temptation was my heart's desire.

Go away. I won't stray.

The flesh can become weak with hot breath

Breathing on your neck.

Words of passion being whistled in your ear.

Go away. I won't stray.

My body is my temple.

I guard it. I respect it. I treasure it.

Go away. I won't stray.

When the flesh wouldn't break,

Temptation tried to buy me.

Go away. I won't stray.

If by chance you find a great love, a real love,

. . . .

119

And you find yourself counting lovers, not
love—

Tell temptation:

Go away. I won't stray.

HERO

I went looking for a hero but found myself
a zero.

Oh, what a waste. I was fooled by a man.

Had twinkles and stars in my eyes.

No, no, not a hero, but a zero.

He was promising me the world.

Grinning from cheek to cheek. I was smiling
and profiling.

No, no, not a hero, but a zero.

Playing booboo, the fool that's me.

No, no, not a hero, but a zero.

I put all my trust, dreams, and hopes in this
man. My love was strong.

No, no, not a hero, but a zero.

Where did I go wrong?

I put this man before God as if he was my
hero.

Now look at me. Crying with my body
wringing.

Realizing I don't have a hero but a zero.

No, no, not a hero, but a zero.

. . . .

After admitting what I had, I had to let go of that zero.

I am no longer looking for a superhero because God is my hero.

No man can stand in God's place.

Don't miss out on God the hero. He is the maker of souls.

The ruler of kingdoms. He is almighty but gentle.

With his breath, life being. Oh, what a hero he is.

The world bends when he calls.

His presence is light. His presence is overwhelming.

No, no, not a hero, but a superhero.

A Man

I always hear women saying they are praying
for a man,

But they have lost sight of what man.

I need the man named Jesus.

An earthly man can make your blood boil

And have you feeling like you are on fire.

That is nothing but desire.

I need the man named Jesus.

We as women love a man all big and strong.

My man smells like a man. I know that
smell anywhere.

I can sniff him out of any crowd.

I need the man named Jesus.

When a woman is in love with a man, she
sees no faults.

They call that the power of love.

I need the man named Jesus.

I've been with my man for years, but I was
still missing something.

It took me years to figure out

That the man I long for wasn't even here on
Earth.

. . . .

I need the man named Jesus.

Once I got my eyes set on the right man and
made my commitment,

Jesus took control of life and love.

He put everything in the right place. Even
gave me a burning love.

Got myself a saved earthly man given to me
by Jesus.

Oh, what a man, who only plays second to
Jesus.

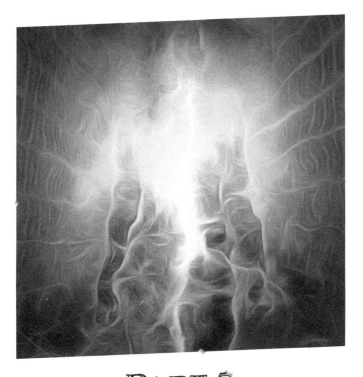

PART 7:
Healings

YOU SHALL LIVE

It is funny how Jesus works.

I saw Jesus on the side of a road.

The road was not straight. I had to go
around a bend.

There stood Jesus healing a blind man.

Saying, "You shall live. Rise up and walk."

I looked ahead; the people were standing in
line.

Jesus was on a healing spree.

Next person was a crippled man.

Jesus laid his hands on the man's knee.

Saying, "You shall live. Rise up and walk."

Here came a woman with her dead child in
her arms.

The woman laid the dead child in Jesus's arms.

Upon the touch of his flesh and with Jesus

Saying, "You shall live. Rise up and walk,"

The child jumped down and ran into the
arms of her mother.

Farther on down the road, I heard a woman
spreading the word that Jesus was on his
way.

. . . .

The woman was shouting,

"The Messiah is here and is moving this way.

He is healing the people on his way."

Jesus is speaking life and healing with these words by

Saying, "You shall live. Rise up and walk."

I got in line. I wanted Jesus to speak life and healing into me.

I was willing to accept his healing and his offer of life.

I saw Jesus on the side of a road.

KNOW YOUR PLACE

In the Bible, it says a man is the head of the
household.

A woman came from his rib.

Know your place; keep living.

The world is changing so fast. Makes no
sense to me.

We have forgotten all our teachings from the
Bible.

Know your place; keep living.

Our lives are spinning out of order.

Women stepping in to be the man.

Kids not knowing who they are.

I need a man to step back in.

Know your place; keep living.

When you can't follow God's orders,

who orders are we following?

I need an old-soul man who wants to lead.

My life depends on it. Keep me from
messing up.

Know your place; keep living.

I don't want to lead, never have.

. . . .

I am a part of you.

I came from your body as a rib. Check your ribs; one's missing.

Know your place; keep living.

I am your wife, the mother of your children.

I am your playmate and lover. Feed me and guide me.

Know your place; keep living.

Let's get real with this.

I need a strong, saved man to guide me.

I will stand right beside you.

When you are up, I am up. When you are down, I am down.

Know your place; keep living.

As I always say, "Can a real man stand up and guide me?"

Know your place; keep living.

GONE MISSING

If I died today, someone would surely miss me.

All that I was would be gone.

I went missing. Lost and unfound.

What role did I play?

I was a mother, sister, niece, and aunt.

Please don't forget that I was someone's friend.

But most of all, I was someone's wife.

I went missing. Lost and unfound.

When a change comes over a person,

The old you may have to die for the new you to begin.

I went missing. Lost and unfound.

The old me was wicked and unsaved.

The old me didn't know Jesus.

The old me stayed in trouble.

I went missing. Lost and unfound.

When I found Jesus, I was made anew.

My family and friends didn't recognize me.

They started looking for me.

. . . .

I went missing. Lost and unfound.

I had to set aside my old ways to adopt my new ways.

I was still me but not me.

I tried to tell my family and friends

That it was still me and that I was still here,

But no one could hear me.

I went missing. Lost and unfound.

The moral of this story is sometimes

You must lose you to find you.

It is okay to make a change in your life for the better.

Go missing; lose yourself. Start a new beginning with Jesus.

I went missing. Lost and unfound.

No Mercy

With some people, it is easy to give up on
life.

They will take their own life with no mercy
from this world.

This world holds no hostages. Life is its
bargaining tool.

No mercy. I want to live.

When you get beat up by this world

You must go deep within yourself to find
yourself.

You've got to hold yourself and cuddle
yourself.

No mercy. I want to live.

Say it to yourself.

This body is on borrowed time, and I need
more time.

You must put what is going on in this world
behind you.

Check your rearview mirror.

No mercy. I want to live.

Jesus instilled the breath of life in you.

If your breath is getting short,

. . . .

Don't rip open your chest crying out for
more air.

Trust me, Jesus will inflate you with more
air.

No mercy. I want to live.

Jesus will light a fire under you by telling
you,

"Don't get caught up in this world." No
mercy will be given.

You must choose life.

No mercy. I want to live.

Don't fall short due to the meanness of this
world.

There is a better world that you should be
looking forward to

called Paradise.

Suicide is never the right answer.

Call somebody.

Have mercy. I want to live.

BREAKTHROUGH

It looks like life was turning against me.

I was stressed and under pressure.

My mind was working against me.

I'm praying for a breakthrough.

I went down on my knees, calling on the
name of Jesus.

When I pray, I pray for real.

I'm praying for a breakthrough.

I said, "Jesus, I need your strength.

My mind, my body is failing me.

Something is overpowering me."

I'm praying for a breakthrough.

I was being turned inside out.

I didn't know which way was up.

I'm praying for a breakthrough.

My friends were dropping by the wayside.

It hard to stand by someone who is strong.

I'm praying for a breakthrough.

I had to fall back on Jesus.

I always pray, "Lord, let this old body hold
up,

. . . .

and please let my mind stay intact."
I'm praying for a breakthrough.
I know whatever my problem may be,
God always sees me through it.
I'm praying for a breakthrough.

NAME UNKNOWN

Sadness overcame me. My heart was
breaking.

Out of the darkness came forward the light.

Out of the hatred came forward the love.

I need a miracle worker. Yes, I do.

In sickness, in health, I got to make it to the
end.

I need a miracle worker. Yes, I do.

I heard the news. There was a miracle
worker on the loose.

I asked what the miracle worker's name was.

The stranger stated, "Name unknown."

I need a miracle worker. Yes, I do.

I stated, "That's okay, because I can
recognize him when I see him.

I know his voice. I know his name. The man
called Jesus is his name."

I need a miracle worker. Yes, I do.

I advised the stranger,

"Don't you fret over his name.

He is known by his works."

I need a miracle worker. Yes, I do.

. . . .

It is he who can bring the dead back to life.

Even he rose from the dead.

I need a miracle worker. Yes, I do.

When the miracle worker approached, the crowd shouted,

"What is your name?"

Jesus gazed into the crowd. Jesus stated, "Name unknown, but known by many. You can call me Jesus, the miracle worker."

I said, "Jesus, you, the miracle worker, I need a miracle.

Can you heal me? My soul is dying. My soul is dying.

I need a miracle. Can you heal me?"

Jesus looked at me. Jesus said,

"It is already done. By your faith, you are healed. Your soul is saved with me."

"Unknown name" was made known. Jesus, the miracle worker.

· · · · · · · · · ·

I Heard

Have you heard from Jesus? Someone told me he went missing.

I started panicking. I've got to sound the alarm.

Alert! Alert! I'm looking for Jesus.

I said, "That can't be."

If Jesus is missing, trouble will be coming my way.

Alert! Alert! I've got to find Jesus.

I went looking for Jesus. I left no stone unturned. I start shouting his name.
Calling, "Jesus, where are you?"

His voice rose to my call.

Jesus said, "My child, I am answering your call."

I said, "Jesus, I got scared. Someone told me you went missing."

Jesus told me he had to go see his Father on behalf of this old world. Jesus said, "This world needs a healing. This world needs me.

I am the savior of souls. My people. These people need me."

I said, "Jesus, I've got to let your people

. . . .
139

know

that Jesus is on the prowl, looking for you."

I sounded the alarm.

Alert! Alert! We are in a state of emergency.

Have you heard Jesus is looking for you?

If you are the receiver of this message,

Answer the call. Don't go missing.

Alert! Alert! Have you heard from Jesus?

INTO PRAYER

I was hot, bothered, and frustrated with the
way my life was going.

I had to go into prayer.

I was lonely and misguided. Looking for
love in all the wrong places.

I had to go into prayer.

My finances were upside down.

Didn't even know where my next meal was
coming from.

I had to go into prayer.

I was young and dumb, trying to be a
follower.

I had to go into prayer.

I was a know-it-all, wouldn't listen to
anybody.

I had to go into prayer.

I was fragile, helpless, and broken.

I had to go into prayer.

I was suffering from a loss and couldn't
move forward.

I had to go into prayer.

I was godless with no hope.

. . . .

I had to go into prayer.

I was focusing on myself and not on Jesus.

I had to go into prayer.

If you have similar issues, try going into prayer,

because on the other side of prayer are healings and blessings.

Try Jesus. These are praying times.

PERFECT

I wanted to be perfect.

Striving to achieve an impossible goal.

I wanted to be perfect.

Perfection was my goal. I wanted to be perfect.

Adam and Eve were my travesty.

Making perfection imperfect with two bites from an apple.

Making my eyes see what I did not want to see.

My ears hear what I did not want to hear.

I wanted to be perfect.

This world can be vicious.

Making me feel small, vulnerable, and all. Had me fearing fear itself.

I wanted to be perfect.

Looking in the mirror, I could see all my flaws.

I wanted to be perfect.

I had to learn the hard way to look within

Because God could see all my flaws.

I wanted to be perfect.

. . . .

Yes, we were molded in the image of God.
Can I be like God?

I wanted to be perfect.

Being like God is not perfect.

We must accept our shortcomings and know
that we are worthy.

No, there is nothing about me that is
perfect, but God loves me anyway.

I wanted to be perfect.

THE COLOR OF MY SOUL

That thing that is within,
that makes you whole,

which I call a soul.

No, I am not perfect,

and all things are not made of
sugar and spice, but

My soul is the making of all things nice.

My soul personifies greatness because it is
within me.

My soul guides me to the light of hope,

which is through Jesus.

My soul is the breath of life from God
Almighty.

therefore, I live

when sometimes, I don't even want to live.

My soul makes me rise.

It tells me to get up because tomorrow
always comes.

Question: What is the color of your soul?

Mine is rainbow

. . . .

145

Because I am not defined by a color.
It is just a part of me.
Colorful souls are a rainbow
The making of beautiful people
No matter the race or color.
Pick a color or several.
Who are you?

Can You See Me?

Close your eyes but not your mind.

I was made in the image of my Maker.

I am strong and profound.

Don't let this be too deep for you.

So, if your mind is not clear

and you cannot see me, please stop reading.

See me for who I am. I am black and beautiful.

I am a woman.

I carry the strength of the great army of the Lord.

That strength could be too powerful for you.

Can you see me?

I want you to open your eyes and mind.

See me for who I am.

Not just the outside of me, but also the
inside of me.

Now, open your eyes.

Can you see me?

. . . .

WHEN THE SAVIOR CALLS

The speaking of a soul that is no longer here.

I know you feel the world has come to an
end,

But keep these words in mind.

When the savior calls, you've got to answer.

There will be no missed calls.

Remember all that I was to you,

and know that Jesus has got me.

Family, I heard a cry from above.

It was Jesus calling my name.

I love my family and friends,

but the call moved me to movement.

I rose and said, "I don't want to go, but I've
got to go.

Jesus is calling my name.

I just got a promotion to be an angel in
Heaven."

When you get lonely, I want you to call my
name.

In a flash of a light, I will be there.

. . . .

You may not see me but know that I am
there.

I will whisper these sweet words to you:

"Lift your eyes toward Heaven,

and the shadow that you see:

that is me watching over you."

May these words comfort you in your hour
of need.

ABOUT THE AUTHOR

Spiritual Inspirations was written by Carol Pugh from her intellectual conservations with Jesus, which were years in the making.

These spiritual inspirations are gifted messages from Jesus with Jesus choosing her as the vessel to reveal his gifted messages by saying, "I have something to say and something to give from above."

Spiritual Inspirations' gifted messages are deep and profound messages that will uplift inspire and motivate your soul.

Spiritual Inspirations' mission is to keep God in the forefront by letting all know that all is not lost.

I hope all the readers enjoyed reading these gifted conversations between me and Jesus as much as I enjoyed writing them.

I truly believe there is something in this book that will touch all souls. Continue to be blessed and let Jesus soothe your soul.

CPSIA information can be obtained
at www.ICGtesting.com
Printed in the USA
JSHW011218100922
30339JS00001B/2